SWU-MED-004

14TH CENT. GERMAN TOURNAMENT KNIGHTS

Luca Stefano Cristini

SOLDIERSHOP PUBLISHING

THE AUTHOR

Luca Stefano Cristini has edited various publications on ancient and contemporary historical themes, including books on thirty years war, Medieval, Napoleonic as well as several illustrated books with historical color photographs. He has also curated all the brands of Soldiershop publishing.

PUBLISHING'S NOTES

LICENSES COMMONS

ACKNOWLEDGEMENTS

A Special Thanks to New York Public Library (NYPL) owner of the original plates of the book that release the Pd with a licence CCO 1.0. Related all our book series in the same brand we thanks to also all the several institution, museum, library, bibliotecks, public or private collection & athenaeums that with their positive copyright policy about part of his collections, allows us the use of many images present in our books. We remember same of this great World Institutions: New York Public Library, Rara CH, Heidelberg Biblioteck University, Riikmuseum of Amsterdam, Dusseldorf University Library, Polona Library, Herzog August Bibliothek of Wolfenbüttel, Stuttgart Bibliothek, SLUB Dresden, Frankfurt am Main Universitätsbibliothek, Europeana, Wikipedia, and many others...

For a complete list of Soldiershop titles please contact Luca Cristini Editore on our website: www.soldiershop.com or www.cristinieditore.com. E-mail: info@soldiershop.com

Title: **14TH Cent. German tournament knights** By Luca Stefano Cristini.
ISBN code: 9788893275392 First edition January 2029 Cover & Art Design: Luca S. Cristini
Published by Luca Cristini Editore for Soldiershop brand via Orio 35/4 - 24050 Zanica (BG) ITALY. www.soldiershop.com

14Th Cent. GERMAN TOURNAMENT KNIGHTS

Luca Stefano Cristini

XIV CENT. GERMAN-SAXON KNIGHTS
IN TOURNAMENTS AND PARADES

This collection of medieval plates, dedicated to Saxon knights in tournament dress from the 14th century, was created in 1889 to celebrate the anniversary of the distinguished Wettin family. The book dates back to 1889 and was printed by Wilhelm Hoffmann of Dresden in a very limited edition of 52 x 38 cm each panel.

The technique used is the chromolithography method, the lithographer is G. Hohneck, who used the collotype technique to colour all the images obtained.

Our very rare copy comes from the plates that belonged to the Dutch doctor H. J. Vinkhuijzen, an eccentric collector and passionate lover of military iconography. Since 1911 the collection has been donated to the New York Public Library by Mr. Henry Draper, heir to the Dutch doctor.

And it is from this collection that Soldiershop has taken the subjects of this new publication.

Almost all the original images were in a bad state of preservation, full of stains, scratches and rips on all the pictures. For our book we have submitted each table to a rigorous cleaning and re-classification to provide a complete, easy and useful work for all scholars and fans of uniformology of military history, costume and beyond.

The **House of Wettin** is a dynasty of German counts, dukes, prince-electors and kings that once ruled territories in the present-day German states of Saxony, Saxony-Anhalt and Thuringia.

The dynasty is one of the oldest in Europe, and its origins can be traced back to the town of Wettin, Saxony-Anhalt. The Wettins gradually rose to power within the Holy Roman Empire. Members of the family became the rulers of several medieval states, starting with the Saxon Eastern March in 1030. Other states they gained were Meissen in 1089, Thuringia in 1263, and Saxony in 1423. These areas cover large parts of Central Germany as a cultural area of Germany. The family divided into two ruling branches in 1485 by the Treaty of Leipzig: the Ernestine and Al-

◄ Henry the illustrious, Margrave of Meißen and Landgrave of Thuringia, one of the main protagonists of the Wettin house depicted in the Codex Manesse, 13th century

bertine branches. The older Ernestine branch played a key role during the Protestant Reformation.

Many ruling monarchs outside Germany were later tied to its cadet branch, the House of Saxe-Coburg and Gotha. The Albertine branch, while less prominent, ruled most of Saxony and played a part in Polish history.

Agnates of the House of Wettin have, at various times, ascended the thrones of Great Britain, Portugal, Bulgaria, Poland, Saxony, and Belgium. Only the British and Belgian lines retain their thrones today.

Collotype is a dichromate-based photographic process invented by Alphonse Poitevin in 1856, and used for large-volume mechanical printing before the introduction of cheaper offset lithography.

It can produce results difficult to distinguish from metal-based photographic prints because of its microscopically fine reticulations which compose the image. Many old postcards are collotypes.

Its possibilities for fine art photography were first employed in the United States by Alfred Stieglitz. The collotype plate is made by coating a plate of glass or metal with a substrate composed of gelatin or other colloid and hardening it. Then it is coated with a thick coat of dichromated gelatin and dried carefully at a controlled temperature (a little over 50° Celsius) so it "reticulates" or

▲ Frederick I, Margrave of Meissen, Landgrave of Thuringia and Count Palatine of Saxony. Romanticist 19th-century painting from the Albrechtsburg in Meißen.

breaks up into a finely grained pattern when washed later in approximately 16 °C water.

The plate is then exposed in contact with the negative using an ultraviolet (UV) source which changes the ability of the exposed gelatin to absorb water later.

The plate is developed by carefully washing out the dichromate salt and dried without heat. The plate is left in a cool dry place to cure for 24 hours before using it to print. To produce prints, the plate is dampened with a glycerine–water mixture which is slightly acidic, then blotted before inking with collotype ink using a leather or velvet roller.

A hard-finished paper such as Bristol is then put on top of the plate and covered with a tympan before being printed typically using a hand proof press. Collotypes are printed using less pressure than is used in printing intaglio or stone lithography. While it is possible to print by hand using a roller or brayer, an acceptable consistency of pressure and even distribution of ink is most effectively achieved using a pres.

Because of its ability to print fine detail, it was also used for business cards and invitations with fine script lettering.

CAVALIERI SASSONI IN TENUTA DA TORNEO E TRIONFO NEL XIV SECOLO

Questa raccolta di tavole medievali, dedicate a cavalieri sassoni in tenuta da torneo del XIV secolo è stata realizzata nel 1889 per celebrare l'anniversario dell'illustre famiglia dei Wettin.

La Casata di Wettin, dal nome Witzel modificatosi nel tempo, fu una dinastia tedesca di conti, duchi, principi elettori (Kurfürsten) e re che governarono l'area corrispondente allo stato della Sassonia per più di ottocento anni. Discendenti della Casata di Wettin, in varie epoche, ascesero ai troni di Gran Bretagna, Portogallo, Bulgaria, Polonia, Sassonia e Belgio; di questi, solo la linea britannica (Windsor) e quella belga (Sassonia-Coburgo-Gotha) regnano ancora.

La stampa del libro risale appunto al 1889 ed è stata eseguita dall'editore Wilhelm Hoffmann di Dresda in tiratura molto limitata nel formato di 52 x 38 cm ogni tavola.

La tecnica utilizzata è quella della cromolitografia, autore delle tavole il litografo G. Hohneck, che utilizzando la tecnica della collotipia ha colorato tutte le immagini ricavate.

La nostra copia, rarissima, deriva dalle tavole appartenute al collezionista e medico olandese H. J. Vinkhuijzen, collezionista eccentrico e appassionato cultore di iconografia militare. Dal 1911 la collezione è stata donata alla New York Public Library dal sig. Henry Draper erede del medico olandese. Ed è da questa collezione che Soldiershop ha preso i soggetti di questa nuova pubblicazione. Quasi tutte le immagini originali si presentavano in un penso stato di conservazione, pieni di macchie, graffi e strappi su tutte le immagini. Per il nostro libro abbiamo sottoposto ogni tavola ad una una rigorosa pulizia e ri-classificazione per fornire un'opera completa, agevole e utile per tutti gli studiosi e gli appassionati di uniformologia di storia militare e costume e non solo.

La collotipia, un'arte ormai scomparsa

Questa particolare tecnica prevede che su di una matrice, costituita da una lastra di cristallo, venga steso uno strato uniforme di emulsione fotosensibile, che deve essere successivamente sottoposta a cottura per alcune ore per poter essere impressionata dal negativo fotografico dell'immagine da stampare. Segue poi l'inchiostratura manuale a spatola, che permette di mantenere un costante aggiornamento sulla quantità e sui toni del colore. L'intensità e i contrasti di colore sono determinati invece dal diverso grado di sviluppo della lastra, modificabile anche durante il procedimento di stampa.

La collotipia permette di stampare da ciascuna matrice soltanto un numero limitato di copie (la tiratura ottimale è tra le 300 e le 500 copie da ciascuna lastra). Dopo una certa quantità di passaggi, infatti, la gelatina si deteriora facendo perdere all'immagine la sua incisività.

▲ Friedrich III of Thuringia, (1332- 1381), Landgrave of Thuringia and Margrave of Meissen, was the son of Frederick II, Margrave of Meissen and Mathilde of Bavaria. From a painting from Albrechtsburg in Meißen.

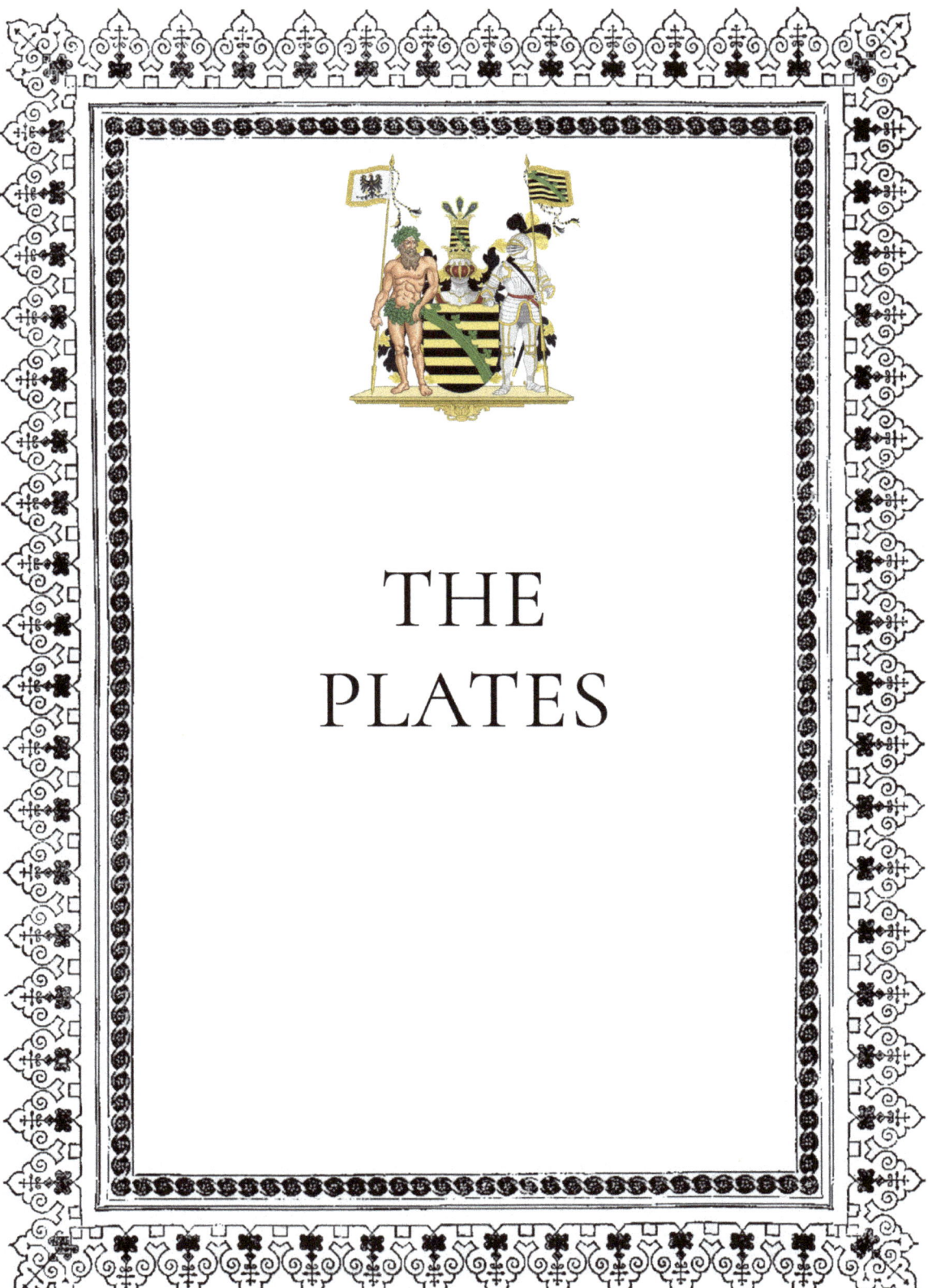

THE
PLATES

TITOLI PUBBLICATI - ALREADY PUBLISHING

SWU-MED-004